B.C.
rides again

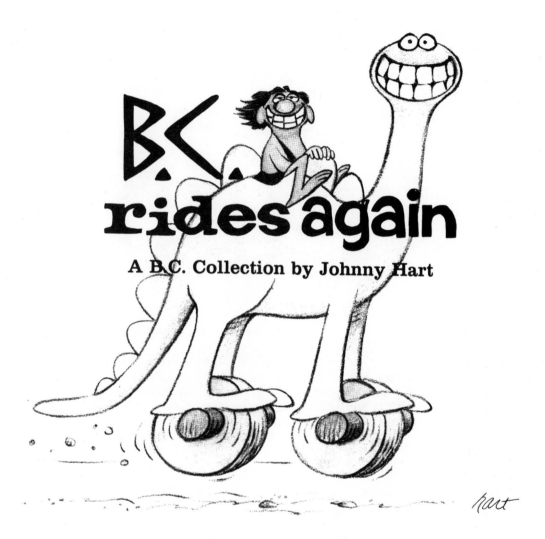

B.C. rides again

A B.C. Collection by Johnny Hart

Andrews and McMeel
A Universal Press Syndicate Company
Kansas City • New York

B.C. is syndicated internationally by Creators Syndicate, Inc.

B.C. Rides Again copyright © 1988 by Creators Syndicate, Inc.
All rights reserved. Printed in the United States of America. No
part of this book may be used or reproduced in any manner
whatsoever without written permission except in the case of
reprints in the context of reviews. For information write
Andrews and McMeel, a Universal Press Syndicate Company,
4900 Main Street, Kansas City, Missouri 64112.

ISBN: 0-8362-1803-5

Library of Congress Catalog Card Number: 87-73259

First Printing, March 1988
Second Printing, December 1988

—————— ATTENTION: SCHOOLS AND BUSINESSES ——————

Andrews and McMeel books are available at quantity discounts with
bulk purchase for educational, business, or sales promotional use. For
information, please write to: Special Sales Department, Andrews and
McMeel, 4900 Main Street, Kansas City, Missouri 64112.

Dear Fat Broad, I am in a dither

I weigh 5 pounds less than my twin sister. She weighs 103 pounds. What should I do?

1·10

YOU CAN **BOTH** DROP DEAD!

MY LATEST INVENTION, "THE BELL"

WHAT'S WITH THE LITTLE PAIR OF HANDS?

THAT'S THE CLAPPER!

1·25

DO YOU BELIEVE IN REINCARNATION?

YES

WHAT WOULD YOU LIKE TO COME BACK AS?

PRACTICALLY ANYTHING.

3·3

9

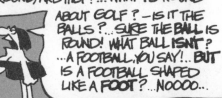

inheritance tax

WILEY'S DICTIONARY

THE coup de grâce DELIVERED BY THE I.R.S.

. . . . hart

SWAHILI

WILEY'S DICTIONARY

THE LANGUAGE USED BY THE NATIONAL ENQUIRER TO PRINT THEIR RETRACTIONS.

. . . . hart

prime numbers

WILEY'S DICTIONARY

HUGH HEFNER'S TELEPHONE DIRECTORY.

. . . . hart

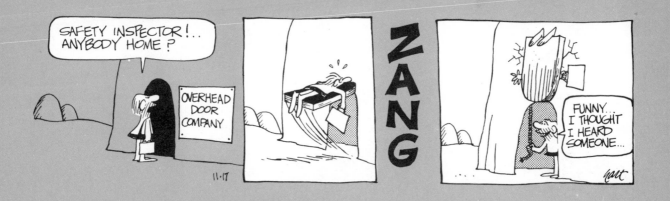

21

27

Flail:

1-23

the opposite of slucceed

WILEY'S
DICTIONARY

I'D LIKE A RINGSIDE SEAT FOR WHEN THE SWALLOWS COME BACK TO CAPISTRANO.

TICKETS

5·11

I'M AFRAID THAT ONE'S ALL BOOKED UP.

HOW 'BOUT FOR WHEN THE GRACKLES DE-BUS IN ALTOONA?

TICKETS

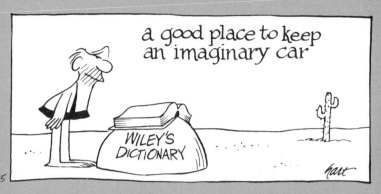

Dear Fat Broad,

what can I do to keep my wife from going out on me?!

7-23

STICK HER BIG TOE IN A LIGHT SOCKET.

hart

WHAT HAS FOUR LEGS, A TAIL AND SURRENDERS?

I GIVE UP.

8-1

..AW, FER CRYIN' OUT LOUD!

hart

null and void

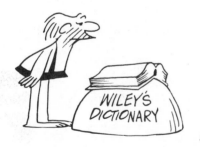

DOWN and DIRTY

WHAT YOU GET WHEN YOU 'MUD WRESTLE' A DUCK

de·light

WHAT A REFRIGERATOR DOES WHEN YOU CLOSE THE DOOR

Bloodless Coup

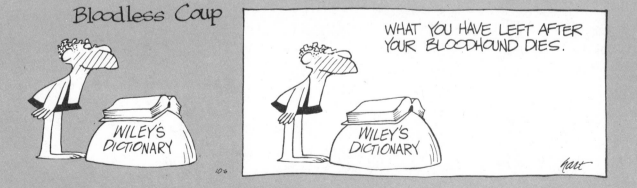

WHAT YOU HAVE LEFT AFTER YOUR BLOODHOUND DIES.

nose drops

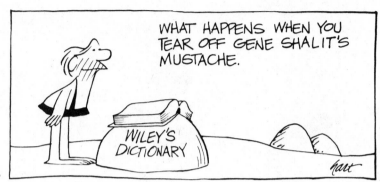

42

43

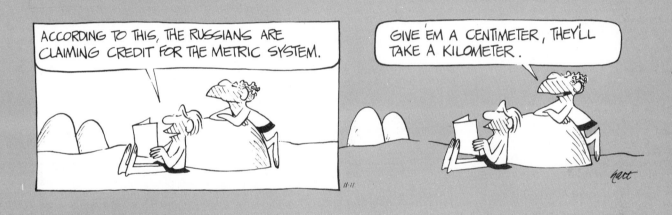

45

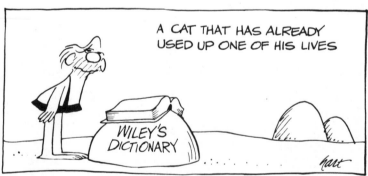

49

I'M SORRY, THE SHELL YOU HAVE SELECTED IS A 'NON-ROARING' SHELL.   PLEASE SELECT ANOTHER SHELL AND TRY AGAIN.

IF THERE **IS** A GOD, GIVE ME SOME SORT OF SIGN !

ZOT

...THAT WAS NOSTALGIC

60

pres·ti·dig·it·ator

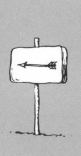

YOU'RE KIDDING!

THOR BOUGHT ONE.

HOW DID HE LIKE IT?

I DON'T KNOW. ...HE NEVER COULD GET HIS FACE OUT OF HIS MOUTH.

SOUR PICKLES

5·17

SOUR PICKLES

pastoral scene

WILEY'S DICTIONARY

5·18

WHAT THE REVEREND GOES THROUGH WHEN HE COMES HOME LATE.

WILEY'S DICTIONARY

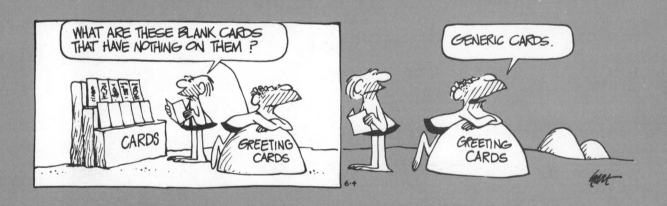

Dear Fat Broad,

What do you do with a husband that has lousy taste?

COUNT YOUR BLESSINGS.

HOW ARE YOUR TOMATOES TODAY?

I'LL CHECK.

TOMATOES

HOW YOU DOIN'?

S'AWRIGHT!

TOMATOES

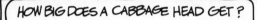

Dear Fat Broad,

Is it permissible to pierce a baby's ears?

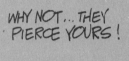

WHY NOT... THEY PIERCE YOURS!

HOW FAR BACK DO YOU GO, GRAMPS?

ALL THE WAY TO MY TAIL!

HA HA HA HA HA

I SWORE TO HECK I WOULD NEVER ASK HIM THAT AGAIN!

WHIFF
WHIFF
WHIFF
WHIFF

DO I GET A 'BASE ON BROADS' FOR THAT?....

4·4

OK, KID, IF YOU GET ON BASE, I WANT YOU TO STEAL SECOND.

STEAL SECOND?

...JUST DON'T TELEGRAPH IT BY TAKING A BIG LEAD OFF FIRST, OK?

4·5

I THINK I KNOW WHY WE'RE 0 AND 75.

LOOK, DAD, A FISH WITH A $3.75 STICKER ON HIS BACK.

GET AWAY FROM THERE, SON!

4·27

WHY, THOSE STINKING CREEPS!... THEY MARKED ME DOWN FROM $6.95

Grandstand play:

TRYING TO PICK UP A CHICK WITH A CUP OF BEER AND A BAG OF PEANUTS.

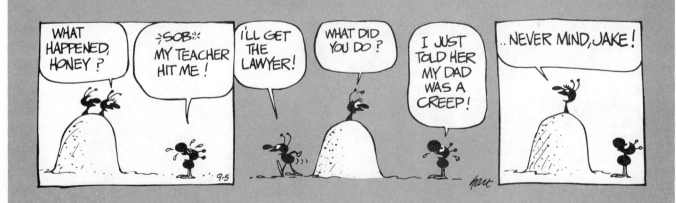

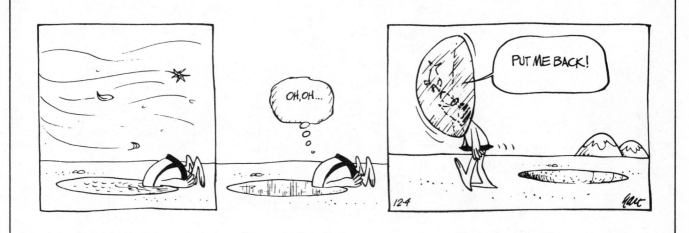

99

trivia pursuit

1.23

1.25

re·bus

GET BACK ON THE

Tusc·a·loosa

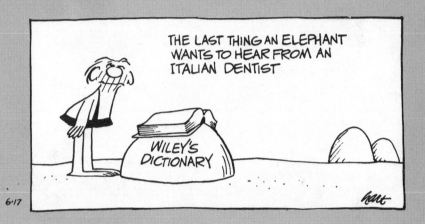

THE LAST THING AN ELEPHANT
WANTS TO HEAR FROM AN
ITALIAN DENTIST

IT'S NO USE, MILDRED,
I'M RUNNING AWAY
WITH SHIRLEY!

...WE SAIL TODAY ON THE TITANIC!

I HOPE IT SINKS!

gum·line

THE SHORTEST DISTANCE
BETWEEN YOUR MOUTH AND
THE BOTTOM OF A SEAT

WILEY'S
DICTIONARY

7·29

WHAT KIND OF JOINT **IS** THIS?...
WHY AREN'T THE RESTROOMS MARKED?

...OH, WELL,... I HAVE A DENTAL
APPOINTMENT TOMORROW ANYWAY...

WILEY'S
BAR

8·5

117

118

la·goon